LIVING

WITH

ST FRANCIS

A WEEK OF PRAYER

AND MEDITATION

FRANCISCAN
PUBLISHING

Living with St Francis: A Week of Prayer and Meditation
First edition 2024

Published by The Franciscan Publishing Company Ltd,
Darlington, Co. Durham, England.

ISBN 9781915198167

Cover design by Sadie Butterworth-Jones

Printed by Newton Press, Blue Bridge Centre,
St Cuthbert's Way, Newton Aycliffe DL5 6DS,
on sustainably sourced paper and card,
using vegetable based inks on a waterless printing press.

FSC

Cover image is that said to be painted on the coffin lid of St Francis and is used with permission and in gratitude to the Museum of the Porziuncola in Assisi. Full image on inside back cover.

Contents

INTRODUCTION

The radical combination of a life of poverty allied with a fervent joy in proclaiming the Gospel made St Francis a centre of attention during his lifetime and continues to draw millions of people to Assisi each year who are intrigued by his personality. I count myself among those who were attracted and affected by the magnetism of this saint, which in my case led to me leaving my home country of Ireland, joining the Order of the Friars Minor and living here in his birthplace for many years, becoming a member of the very Province which began the Order back at the start of the thirteenth century. It is from this experience that I draw the material for this book, which is not an attempt to add to the erudite studies of the life of the Saint, but rather an attempt to convey the spirit of Francis and the Franciscan spirituality which has been handed down to the present generation of friars.

There is an Irish proverb which runs 'Ní h-eolas go h-aontíos', which means that you do not really know someone until you live with them. Just living in Assisi, staying in the friaries where Francis lived and prayed, and walking in his footsteps through the countryside of Umbria and surrounding regions, gives a sense of who this man, who lived back in the thirteenth century, was and how he is still relevant today. For even if Francis died back on 3rd October 1226, his spirit lives on and can still be felt here in the heart of Italy.

Living with St Francis

A second way in which Francis can be encountered is through his own writing and then through those of his biographers, who began very shortly after his death to set down for posterity the remarkable life of this saint. St Jerome said that an ignorance of the Scriptures amounted to ignorance of Jesus Christ, and it would certainly be true to say that failing to read the Franciscan sources would necessarily entail a lack of knowledge about Francis. Of course, these sources should be treated with discernment. There are first of all the authentic writings of St Francis himself, from those in his own hand, such as the *Blessing for Brother Leo* and the *Praises to God the Most High*, together with those dictated by him, like his various letters and the *Canticle of the Creatures*; then there are the biographies written about him by contemporaries who had access to first hand evidence in respect of the life of the Saint; and finally there are stories written about him much later in time, most notably the *Little Flowers of St Francis*, which may be less reliable in respect of eyewitness evidence but preserve what may be described as a folk memory of the Franciscan movement. Although in this book I will not be citing with footnotes the sources from which examples are taken, all references to the stories are taken from the official Italian Franciscan Sources (*Fonti Francescane*), to comply with the admonition of St Bonaventure, a later Minister General of the Order, who wished to avoid the friars recounting unfounded tales.

The handing down of traditions and memories through the centuries is not to be taken lightly. The Franciscan Order may have grown from the seed which Francis planted at the start of the thirteenth century but the links have been maintained with the origins, not alone in respect of the friaries which date back to those times, but also the prayer and devotion which Francis enjoined on the friars and which they continue to this day. The Franciscans have the same Rule, approved by Pope Honorius III

Introduction

in 1223, and apart from the prayer and fasting enjoined by this norm, they also pray using the words of St Francis in various forms. This is the third way of coming into contact with the spirit of Francis and will be used in this book. Each day commences with a prayer invoking the Holy Spirit and ends with a further prayer taken from the current Franciscan Prayer book used in the Umbrian Province, translated from the Italian by myself.

I have designed this book in the form of a week-long retreat. It could be seen as being divisible in two parts. In the first, comprising the first three days, the story of Francis is recounted through his conversion, vocation and prayers; in the second part, comprising the remaining four days, the Franciscan charism is analysed in light of the places which symbolise so many of its aspects, and then through a closer look at three central columns of the charism, in terms of the Catholic faith, the feminine influence and the Cross. Someone having the good fortune to come to Umbria can visit the places which are mentioned in the text, but it is not necessary to come here to feel the spirit of Francis. Francis simply founded his Order here and sent it out to the whole world to preach the Good News of Jesus Christ. The friars were not bound to Assisi. They were itinerants and Francis gave directions in his letters, admonitions and Testament, not alone to the friars that he knew in Italy but to those who would join the Order and live in all parts of the world — not only in the thirteenth century but right until the end of the world. One can meet Francis therefore anywhere in the world at any time, and that encounter is almost always life changing.

Friar Eunan
Assisi
May 2024

DAY ONE

CONVERSION

Invocation of the Holy Spirit

Come, O Consoler,
and pour oil and wine upon our old wounds.
From the kingdom of darkness,
guide us to the source of that first Eternal Love.
Wash away our sins,
transform us into the beginning of a new creation.
O Consoling Spirit, wedding gift and source of every real good,
give daily harmony and perfect joy to the Church of Christ.

Amen.

'In the beginning was the Word and the Word was with God and the Word was God' is the profound opening proclamation of the Gospel of St John. For all Christians it is this encounter with the Word that changes their lives from darkness to light, a process that may be called conversion. The story of the various conversions of the apostles and first disciples are told in the New Testament, from the call of the first apostles to that of St Paul, whose spectacular conversion on the road to Damascus is recalled in the Acts of the Apostles. The Church grows through the witness of the Apostles from Pentecost onwards. On that day it was the Word preached by Peter that cut to the heart those who listened and led to three thousand people being baptised on that one day, marking that change in their lives whereby Christ is put at the centre. So what is the story of St Francis' conversion?

I look at it from three perspectives. The first is from the point of view of listening to the Word, just as the first converts did at Pentecost. Francis, of course, was born into a Catholic family, baptised according to tradition in the cathedral of San Rufino in Assisi. However it is clear from his biographies that Francis for the first part of his life very much belonged to the world. He wished to be at the centre, dressing to attract attention and forming a group of friends around himself of which he was clearly the leader. His dream was to become a knight, to be the conquering warrior and to belong to the most powerful class in the society of the times, the nobility. But all his dreams floundered on the rocks of reality. He went to war, but in his first battle he landed on the losing side and spent a year in prison before being ransomed by his father. He tried to set off once again to fulfil his dreams of a castle, followers, fame and glory but had to turn back from the military campaign because he accepted the voice in his dream that he had been following a servant and not the master. Bereft of his illusions he came then to the little church of San Damiano where, at the age of twenty-four, he was at last ready to listen to the voice of God. That instruction was clear — he was to rebuild the church, which he could see was falling down. Many interpreters have opined that Francis misunderstood the message, that it was not the physical building that was to be repaired but the spiritual body of the Church, but I think there is much to be said for the view that the latter was not the exclusive reason. The Lord could quite rightly have been saying to Francis

Conversion

to forget about seeking superiority, taking up tools that are designed for destruction, and turn to the humble way of working with his hands and building instead. He did not forget the instruction and emphasises in his Testament that he, himself, used to work with his hands and that he still desired to do so, and he enjoined on his brothers the firm command that they may give themselves to honest work. Because it is, of course, not enough to simply listen to the Word; it is necessary to put what you have listened to into practice, otherwise as the New Testament reminds us, in the letter of James, we would be like a person who looks into a mirror and then forgets his own reflection. Francis believed in putting the Gospel that he heard into practice without a gloss on it. When he heard the Gospel of Matthew describing the apostolic mission that Jesus sent them upon without gold, or silver or copper, he declared that it was exactly what he desired to do and longed for and immediately set about putting it into practice.

The description of Francis' conversion, from a second perspective, is told in his own words in the opening words of his Testament:

> The Lord granted me, Brother Francis, to begin to do penance in this way. While I was in sin, it seemed too bitter to me to look upon lepers, but the Lord himself led me among them and I had mercy on them. And when I left them that which seemed bitter to me was turned into sweetness of soul and body; and afterward I lingered a little and left the world.

The encounter with the leper could be described as the turning point in Francis' life and this is how he looks upon it himself because he does not recount in his Testament anything of the miraculous episode of a crucifix that spoke to him, or indeed how he put the command of rebuilding the Church into action. The moment that changed his life was when, instead of running away from that which he most feared, the leper, he overcame his repugnance and fear and embraced the person that stood in front of him. The leper, of course, was the very opposite of a handsome, noble knight — he was a person who was sick, disfigured by the disease he had contracted, at the very margins of human society and consigned to death. But in spiritual terms Francis, before his conversion, may be described in those very terms. He was consumed by his own ambitions, not concerned for the welfare of others; directed by his own will, rather than by God's and, as a result, disfigured by sin rather than reflecting God's light. His action in embracing the leper was a reflection of Christ embracing him.

Whereas conversion in ordinary terms may be considered as a turning away from one path to another on a horizontal axis, it may also be seen paradoxically on the vertical axis as a fall, or a turning upside down. This is the ultimate perspective. In one film about St Francis he is standing on his head looking at the city of Assisi, a point of view which, as G.K. Chesterton notes in his biography of St Francis, emphasises dependence. In one sense it is the wrong way round but in another Francis is seeing a reality that only God's providence is keeping this town built on a rock hanging on to the earth. A reference has already been made to the conversion of St Paul, who is immortalised in the Caravaggio painting, falling from his horse, even though there is no reference in the Acts of the Apostles as to whether he was in fact mounted on any steed at all. Francis did have a horse and certainly fell from it, at least in a metaphorical way, when he was captured in battle. He then became a prisoner as opposed to a free man. From horseman and would-be knight he became a 'fool' for God, or *jongleur de Dieu*, in the French language which he loved. The point is, however, that he embraced this role, for he had discovered the truth which would be expressed in the words of one of his earliest followers, the Blessed Brother Giles, that if you want to hear you must be deaf, if you want to see you must be blind, and if you want to go up you must go down. Those are precisely the aspects of conversion which are to be meditated upon.

Jesus, quoting the prophet Isaiah, explains to his disciples why he speaks to the people in parables, so that whilst seeing they do not perceive and hearing they do not understand. The purpose of such hearing and seeing is that we convert and are healed from what ails us. It is a matter of life or death then that we indeed do hear the Word of God and are deaf to the noise and murmurings of this world. It is a matter of life or death that we indeed see in the hungry, the thirsty, the naked, the sick, the stranger and the prisoner, the Christ who wishes us to embrace us to himself and to give us his healing touch. It is a matter of life or death that we choose a path that seems to lower us more and more than one which raises us up, because it is only God who can lift us to the higher place to which he wishes to take us, and the illusion that we can do it for ourselves will shatter as it did for Francis if we pursue it. Francis experienced for himself our wretched and parlous state but he found a way out of it — the only Way — he called on Jesus Christ. He saw him in the leper, he listened to his Word and he experienced his healing grace. There is a difference between the word of man and the Word of God. The former you may take or leave, but the Word of God either takes you or leaves you, and it is better of course not to be left.

Concluding Prayer

Response: **Almighty, eternal, just and merciful God.**

Grant that we wretches may, through the power of your Love,
do that which we know you wish us to do,
and to wish that which pleases you. /R

Grant that we, purified from within,
and spiritually enlightened and inflamed by the Holy Spirit,
may be enabled to follow in the footsteps of your Beloved Son,
our Lord Jesus Christ. /R

Grant that we, with the help of your grace alone,
attain unto You, Most High,
Who in perfect Trinity and simple Unity live and reign in glory,
Almighty God for ever and ever. Amen. /R

Day Two

Vocation

Invocation of the Holy Spirit

O Holy Spirit, O Paraclete,
one with the Father and the Son
come down kindly to us
into the depths of our souls.

Let voice and mind be of one accord
in the rhythm of our praise
and may your fire unite us
in one undivided soul.

O light of wisdom,
reveal to us the mystery
of the God who is Trinity, yet one,
the fount of eternal Love.

Living with St Francis

The call of the Kingdom of God is to love. Once Francis had stopped adoring himself, as his early biographers describe his conversion, he had to follow his true vocation. This may be described in many ways: that he was called to do penance; that he was called to rebuild the Church; that he was called to go among lepers and show mercy towards them, or simply in the words of the Rule that he was to follow the holy Gospel of Our Lord Jesus Christ by living in obedience, without anything of his own and in chastity. In this section we will look at each of these descriptions in turn. However, there is one love which Francis followed faithfully throughout his life and to whom he is depicted in the frescoes which look down upon the main altar in the Lower Basilica of St Francis in Assisi, as marrying, and that is, of course, Lady Poverty. Although Francis renounced the possibility of marriage in this world by choosing the religious life, he did not repudiate the ideals of courtly love of a knight for his lady. Indeed the espousal of religious life was to all intents and purposes for Francis his betrothal to Lady Poverty. It is as well to bear this idea in mind when we look at Francis. Even prior to the incidents which marked his conversion, the call from the cross of San Damiano and the encounter with the leper, he had declared to his friends that he was dreaming of marrying the most noble, rich and beautiful lady that had ever been seen. Whereas he gave up on the idea of becoming a knight he never gave up on the ideal of knighthood. That was his motivation and that is what carried him through until the end of his earthly life.

When Francis was at the beginning of his religious life, restoring the church of San Damiano, he wore the habit of a hermit and carried a staff. Upon hearing the words of the Gospel where Christ sends out his disciples to preach, without gold, silver or copper for their purses, nor bag for the journey, nor an extra tunic, nor sandals, nor staff, he declares that this is what he desires and what he longs for with all his heart. Immediately

Vocation

afterwards he designs the habit of the friar, leaving aside his staff, and his sandals, and substituting a cord for his belt. I once heard another friar commenting on the importance of the latter substitution. The belt was used in medieval times to attach a purse for one's money and carry one's identity papers, as well, of course, for carrying a sword. Francis could no longer carry such objects and by so doing was proclaiming to the world that he was no longer a man of war, but a man of peace, no longer a rich man, but a poor one, and no longer a 'someone', but rather a 'nobody'. The poverty of Francis was radical and perhaps reflected most closely that preached by Jesus in the Sermon of the Mount. It meant having no money, having no power, being a member of the oppressed in society and simply relying on God's mercy and providence for one's existence. Francis understood that if the friars held property they would need arms to defend it, and by espousing Lady Poverty they had no need to be in conflict with anyone.

Conversion results from the realisation that we are not living a life that is pleasing to God. As a result of that realisation, the first reaction must be contrition for that state of affairs and an attempt to make amends by practising penance. Francis looked at it in very stark terms as can be seen from the exhortation that he allowed all friars to preach.

> Do penance and produce fruits of penance, because soon we will die... Blessed are those who die whilst doing penance, for theirs is the kingdom of heaven. Woe to those who do not die doing penance, for they are the children of the devil whose works they do and they shall go to the eternal fire.
>
> Later Admonition and Exhortation

The importance then of penance for Francis is clear and a foundation for the Order. Indeed, prior to giving the Order the name of Friars Minor, his band was simply known as the Penitents of Assisi. Francis did extreme penance: he wore the poorest of clothes, he begged for food and he fasted often, doing various 'Lents' during the year. However, there is a temptation in this of imposing one's own will and thus sinning against the body, as Francis himself confesses to having done. Perhaps for this reason Francis, through the Spirit, came up with the concept of minority to describe the essence of what a friar should be. It is in concord with the idea of penance because it involves a renouncing of self-will and the idea of putting oneself before others. It is the spiritual habit which Francis wanted all friars to put on and which he, giving the example, donned himself. As a spiritual master Francis would counsel St Clare against excessive fasting and come to describe the body as *Frate Asino* — Brother Donkey, a humble beast of burden but one which carried Christ and was therefore to be treated with the greatest respect.

A vocation is a call to do something and Francis received his particular call directly from Christ to rebuild the Church. I have already stated my belief that the decision to take the command literally was not a mistake on Francis' part but only the beginning of a lifetime's work to build up the body of Christ. The way that he did this is worthy of note in respect of his attitude to all humankind, the faithful, the prelates and the Pope. After rebuilding the physical structure of San Damiano, Francis began his preaching as a religious, to rebuild the Church made up of the faithful, the individual Christians. He had a simple method for his preaching to the faithful. He exhorted all to praise, bless, honour and adore God Almighty in Trinity and unity and to abstain from evil and persevere in good works until the very end. This went from the common people he met to the rulers of the world, whom he advised by letter not to forget about the Lord and even to have a public announcement of the duty to render praise and thanksgiving to the Lord God. Whilst for the prelates, he emphasised the importance of the necessary reverence to be given to the body and blood of Our Lord Jesus Christ and also to the Scriptures, which were likewise to be kept in decorous places and treated with the utmost respect. As evidenced by the Rule, he also advocated obedience and reverence to the reigning pope and to all of his canonically elected successors. But the call was a universal one. Francis, at the start of his preaching, did not even know how to salute the people, and would say, 'Good Day, good people', before starting to talk, but he writes in his Testament that the Lord himself taught him how to address everyone and the greeting was, 'May the Lord give you peace!' For the rebuilding of the whole Church means restoring the peace that is missing from those hearts that are lacking the Lord.

The vocation to assist the lepers arose, as we have seen, out of Francis' own history and they held a special place in his heart. Not alone did he go amongst them personally and show mercy towards them. He also made it a cornerstone of the early friars' formation that they were to work among the lepers. It was the touchstone of minority and humility, and if a friar could not serve the leper then he could not remain in the Order. Even those of noble rank who wished to enter the Order as postulants were told that they had to go to live amongst and serve the lepers and this was not an easy thing. Lepers were feared and Francis had to reprove a friar who allowed one to accompany him to public places. The rebuke was not taken back but Francis did do penance for the offence he had given to the leper concerned by eating from the same bowl, even though blood ran down from the fingers of the latter into the shared vessel. The most difficult case, according to the *Little Flowers of St Francis*, was of a leper who the friars had given up on as he not alone was repugnant to look at but attacked them with words and blows and blasphemed against Christ and the Virgin Mary. When Francis visited the infirmary where he was housed the friars told him of the situation and he offered to take care of him personally. Despite the leper's scorn that he would not be able to do anything more than the friars had done, Francis washed him and as he did so the leper was cured, not alone of his physical illness but also of his spiritual illness. He felt sincere contrition for his sins, confessed them freely and availed of the sacraments. When a short time later he fell ill again from another illness entirely, he died in a state of grace and according to the story in the *Little Flowers of St Francis* he appeared to the Saint, who was praying in a wood, to announce that he was going to paradise.

When a friar makes his solemn profession he promises to abide by the Rule, which may be summarised in the line:

> The Rule and the life of the Friars Minor is this: to observe the Holy Gospel of Our Lord Jesus Christ, living in obedience, without anything of our own and in chastity.

This may be described as the friar's vocation and it is to this that Francis gave his allegiance. He took seriously the vow of obedience and there are numerous writings that caution against the return to the 'vomit of self-will' or murmuring against a superior and he declares his preference to having a guardian, even were it to be a friar just out of his novitiate, rather than being a guardian himself. Similarly in regard to chastity, this was to be jealously guarded. The friars were not to enter the convents of sisters without the appropriate authorisation and they were not to have suspicious contacts with women. But Francis' way of dealing with such temptation, as recounted once again in the *Little Flowers of St Francis*, strikes us as particularly characteristic of his personality. Unlike St Thomas Aquinas who is said to have taken a firebrand to chase away a woman that was sent to seduce him, Francis converts the seductress by inviting her to a bed of fire and leaping into it himself first! Francis esteems the feminine and it is not surprising that at the centre of his Rule is Lady Poverty, living without anything of one's own. That poverty was radical. Francis did not lay claim to anything and condemned himself when he took satisfaction from the response to his preaching, as what he preached were the Lord's words and not his own and he was to have no credit for them. Similarly he advised his friars that they could only glory in their infirmities and sins for which they were responsible and that where they were praised by the people for their good acts, they should immediately praise God from whom the goodness came. In essence Francis followed the teaching of St Paul, that glory lay in embracing the cross of Christ as his only treasure and it is no surprise that the foundation of Franciscan prayer, which the first friars said when they saw a church, was 'We adore thee, O Christ, and we bless thee, because by thy holy cross thou hast redeemed the world.' That is what we shall look at next.

Concluding Prayer

Response: **Lord Jesus, show me the ways of your most delightful Poverty.**

My Lord, most righteous Jesus,
have mercy on me and my Lady Poverty. /R

I languish for love of her,
nor can I rest without her.
My Lord you know that I am in love with her. /R

I ask you to be marked with this privilege,
I desire to be enriched with this treasure. /R

I beseech you, most poor Jesus,
to be able to possess nothing whatsoever under heaven. /R

DAY THREE

PRAYER

Invocation of the Holy Spirit

Come O Holy Spirit,
send us down from heaven
a ray of your light.

Come Father of the poor,
come giver of gifts,
come light of our hearts.

Perfect consoler,
sweet guest of the soul,
sweetest relief.

In tiredness, rest,
in burning heat, shade,
in weeping, comfort.

O most blessed light
captivate from within
the hearts of your faithful.

Living with St Francis

Without your strength
there is nothing in us,
nothing that is without fault.

Wash that which is dirty,
bathe that which is dry,
heal that which is bleeding.

Bend that which is rigid,
warm that which is frozen,
straighten that which is crooked.

Give to your faithful
who confide alone in You,
Your holy gifts.

Give us virtue and reward,
give us a holy death,
give us eternal life.

It is perhaps true to say that a person only really and truly turns
to God when things are falling apart. Whilst things are going well
in life we can pretty well ignore the deity; once suffering enters
into our lives though, it is a different matter. Francis had his first
major experience of suffering after defeat in battle and enduring
the ignominy of being held in prison in Perugia for ransom. He
appears to have suffered some sort of depression after being
released and although briefly uplifted, when he sought to obtain
military glory again, he had to turn back from Spoleto as a second
time failure in his quest for glory. After that he searched for
solitary places in which to pray, from which he seems to have
found comfort. What he found, for example, in the solitude of a

Prayer

cave near Assisi was 'a treasure', as he confided to a friend who accompanied him but remained outside as Francis prayed. It was this communion with God that was the real treasure he had discovered. He had begun to seek to conform his will to the Divine, as Celano his first biographer says, and he began to seek spiritual rather than worldly wealth and fame. What I intend to do in this chapter is to look at various aspects of Franciscan prayer as typified by Francis and his followers, to look at its development from the first encounter of Francis with the crucifix at San Damiano, through to the Order's prayers today.

The prayer before the cross at San Damiano appears in many manuscripts; a simple version which we say here in Umbria still today runs:

> Most High, glorious God, enlighten the darkness of my heart. Give me right faith, certain hope, perfect love, good sense and wisdom O Lord, so that I may always carry out your holy and true command. Amen.

You can see that it is a petitionary prayer — Francis is asking to have something for himself. They are all perfectly good things, but we shall see that in one sense he develops from this throughout his life, not asking for things at all but simply praising God. After his conversion Francis prayed frequently. One of the first witnesses we have of this is from his first follower Bernardo da Quintavalle, who secretly watches him pray as a guest in his house. In fact, however, the only thing that he says is, 'My God, my God', after rising up in the night when he thought that Bernardo had fallen asleep. From having only one follower, the company increased to twelve by the time of the official founding of the Order in 1209 and within twelve years of that five thousand friars were coming to Assisi to celebrate the Chapter of the Mats, where a certain St Anthony of Padua was in attendance as well. The centrality of prayer appears throughout this time and

Living with St Francis

it was, in fact, in a reply to St Anthony, who proposed to teach the friars theology, that Francis underlines its primary importance.

> It pleases me that you teach sacred theology to the brothers, as long as — in the words of the Rule — you 'do not extinguish the Spirit of prayer and devotion' with study of this kind.

Prayer plays an essential part in the Rule. Chapter three is dedicated to the Office to be said by the friars, according to the rite of the Roman Church, and the substitution of these by the recitation of a number of 'Our Fathers' in respect of lay friars, with instructions on fasting and going out to the world with a message of peace. Because through prayer, putting oneself in the presence of God in silence and out of the way places was essential for Francis, it did not clash with the duty of penance and charity. Francis undertook many 'Lents' during the year, there are three alone mentioned in the Rule and he added personal ones for himself. He also seems to have observed the practice of saints such as St Vincent de Paul who, when an act of charity called him away from his prayer, put that first because the duty of love for neighbour comes above all others, and St John Chrysostom, who urged that priority was to be given to feeding the poor rather than the adorning of altars. Francis too was not against adorning the altar with rich fabrics but gave away a particularly valuable cloth to a woman who was not able to feed her family, warning her, as the cloth merchant's son that he was, not to be cheated on the price for which she sold it. Apart from the directions in the Rule, Francis also wrote many other prayers such as the *Office of the Passion*, the *Praises to Be Said at All Hours*, *A Salutation of the Blessed Virgin Mary*, *A Salutation of the Virtues*, and the *Praises to God the Most High*.

Prayer

The practice of the friars from the very start of their community was to give praise to God and when they saw a church, or a cross, they would bow down and recite:

> We praise you, O Lord, and we bless you here and in all your churches throughout the world, because by your holy cross you have redeemed the world.

And Franciscan prayer and devotion has continued through the Order in many ways, which has echoes in the practices of other religious orders and saints. The seven stages of contemplative prayer explained by one of Francis' first companions, Brother Giles, evokes the seven mansions of St Teresa of Avila. He states that the contemplative life lies in the renunciation of all living creatures for the love of God, seeking only for the higher things, in faithfulness in prayer, in frequent spiritual reading, and unceasing praise directed to God in hymns and canticles. The seven stages are:

Fire — by which he means a sort of light which enters to illuminate the soul.

Unction — which follows, is of the spiritual perfume from which a marvellous aroma emanates as is spoken about in the Canticle of Canticles: 'Draw me: and we will run after thee to the odour of thy ointments.'

Ecstasy — when the soul which has breathed in the perfume, is rapt and taken outside of the body.

Contemplation — follows when the soul, seemingly devoid of the body, contemplates God with wonderful clarity.

Taste — is the marvellous sweetness experienced by the soul in contemplation. Psalm 34:8 speaks of this, 'Taste and see that the Lord is good.'

Living with St Francis

Quiet — occurs when the soul, having tasted that sweetness relaxes in it.

Glory — is the final stage when the soul is invested in peace and filled with immense joy. 'I will be fulfilled when your Glory shall appear' (cf. psalm 17:15). This last stage can only be arrived at says Br Giles via unceasing prayer and ardour of the soul.

And just as the contemplative prayer of the Carmelites finds its equivalent in the Franciscan charism, so there is a Franciscan counterpart to the Dominican rosary. The devotion to Mary, so apparent in Francis' prayers, appears also in the Order by means of a Franciscan rosary which became popular in the fifteenth century. It adds two Joyful Mysteries to those of the Dominicans and two Hail Marys, to make a total of seventy-two, the traditional age of Mary when she was assumed into heaven. But to return to Francis himself, the move from a purely petitionary prayer to one of praise can be seen in his *Praises to God the Most High*, just to quote a part:

> You are love, charity.
> You are wisdom, You are humility; You are patience;
> You are beauty, You are meekness, You are security;
> You are inner peace; You are joy; You are our hope and joy;
> You are justice; You are moderation, You are all our riches.

The conclusion of the *Praises to Be Said at All Hours* concentrates on the goodness of God. It finishes with the lines:

> All-powerful, most holy, most High and supreme God:
> All good, supreme good, totally good, You alone who are good;
> may we give You all praise, all glory, all thanks,
> all honour, all blessing, and all good things.
> So be it. So be it. Amen.

Prayer

Francis also commented, just like St Teresa of Avila, on the quintessential Christian prayer, the Our Father. The festoons which Francis adds to the words of the prayer show the filial love that the Saint espoused. To 'Your Kingdom come', he adds the motive:

> ... that You may reign in us through grace and make us come to Your Kingdom, where there is a clear vision of You, perfect love of You, blessed union with You, everlasting enjoyment of You.

He emphasises the following phrase, 'Your will be done on earth as it is in heaven', with his longest comment, of which I cite only the first part. It echoes the principal Christian commandment:

> ... to the end that we may love You with our whole heart by always thinking of You; with our whole soul by ever desiring You; with our whole mind by directing all our intentions to You, by seeking Your honour in all things; and with all our strength by spending all our powers and senses of body and soul in the service of Your love and in nought else.

It is often said by non-believers that in prayer there is only one person speaking when you pray — by militant atheists that we are simply acting nonsensically and talking to an imaginary friend — but the statement in a deeper sense is true. The only Person that is praying is Jesus Christ, through His Spirit to a Father who always listens. Entering into His prayer we are adopted as His brothers and sisters, which is why we can pray 'Our Father'. Francis had a very public falling out with his father, Pietro di Bernardone, to whom he gave back even the clothing which he was wearing and declared that no longer would he call him 'father' but say only 'Our Father who art in heaven'. It was indeed a repudiation of the world and his earthly father but also a call for a universal brotherhood and sisterhood as one family under God.

Concluding prayer

Response: **Remember your children, Father.**

O Most Holy Father, you know perfectly well
how we are in anguish from many dangers
and only follow your footsteps from afar. /R

Give us strength to resist,
purify us that we may shine,
make us fertile so that we may bear fruit. /R

May the spirit of prayer and grace be poured over us
so that we may have the same humility you have,
observe the same poverty that you embraced,
and merit that love
with which you always loved Christ crucified. /R

DAY FOUR

THE FRANCISCAN CHARISM

Invocation of the Holy Spirit

The Good Shepherd has ascended
to the right hand of the Father.
The little flock remains vigilant
with Mary in the upper room.

From the eternal splendours
the gift of prophecy descends
which consecrates the apostles
as heralds of the Good News.

Come O Divine Spirit
with your holy gifts
and make our hearts
a temple to your glory.

O Light of Wisdom,
reveal to us the mystery
of God three and one,
the source of eternal love.

Living with St Francis

A discussion on the Franciscan charism could take up many hours, days, weeks and even years. In one sense the charism can be simply expressed in the first sentence of the Friars' Rule, which is reflected exactly in the Rule of St Clare for the sisters:

> The rule and the life of the Friars Minor is this: to observe the holy Gospel of our Lord Jesus Christ by living in obedience, without anything of their own and in chastity.

But in another sense the Franciscan charism appears to be so wide that Franciscans can live this essential guide in a multiplicity of ways. Francis himself could not be easily described — was he an itinerant preacher, a troubadour, a *jongleur de Dieu*, a penitent, an ascetic, a contemplative, or one of the many other descriptions that are made of him? Francis had so many facets that he continues to attract people of all faiths and none as you can see from the pilgrims who come to Assisi. Perhaps the best description I have heard of him — given in a homily by an ex-Provincial Minister of this Province — to a group of American friars, is that he was a window onto the Infinite.

However, the character of this discourse from the start has been about experiencing Francis and the Franciscan way of life in the place where Francis lived and drew his breath. When I was a postulant in Monteluco, a friary set on the mountain overlooking the town of Spoleto and the beautiful valley that bears the town's name, we made a pilgrimage on foot to a special place for Franciscans, Greccio. A Franciscan saint, St Camilla Battista da Varano, said that the virtuous walk, the wise run and those in love fly. For readers, since the time is short, I would ask you then to take this flight of imagination over the mountains in central Italy to the Rieti valley, not only travelling in space but also in time, back to Christmas Eve of 1223. In a cave there, Francis has arranged for the nativity scene to be recreated and above that scene, Mass will be celebrated with Francis as deacon singing the

The Franciscan Charism

Gospel. As Francis speaks, he seems to bleat the word Bethlehem, and so sweet is the name of Jesus to him that he licks his lips as if they were smeared with honey before pronouncing it. The people have come in a torchlight procession from the towns and villages in the valley and whilst the celebration is ongoing one of them has a vision that the child lying in the manger, who seemed to be dead, has come to life and is breathing once again. This is the Incarnation, Christ living as a man amongst his people, and the reason Franciscans have this devotion of constructing cribs each year at Christmas time. The Franciscan Order springs from the birth of this child.

But a child that is born must grow. It must learn to speak and must learn to love. Francis learns to speak to God in out of the way places, for intimacy with God there must be privacy whether in a simply constructed cell, or a hermitage such as Monteluco, the Speco of Narni, or La Verna. Francis feels that sonship so much that during a night of prayer where one friar has said the Lord's Prayer hundreds of times, Francis has never been able to get beyond those first words 'Our Father'. Children as they grow know that they must obey their parents and listen to what they say. The first commandment is *Shema yisrael!* (Hear, O Israel!) Francis, as we have seen, comes to listen to the Lord's command at the church of San Damiano and goes out from there to rebuild the edifice which is falling into ruin. He rebuilds that church, another called St Peter's, and finally the little church of Our Lady of the Angels at the Portiuncola where he will come to live. Yet it is not enough for Francis to live alone or even in community with his brothers; in order for there to be life there must be a feminine side to the Order. Thus, Francis goes in search of a noble quarry, the young Clare of Assisi who will give up her aristocratic heritage to embrace Christ, poor and crucified. She will initiate the community of the Poor Ladies of San Damiano, who will later become the Second Order, named in honour of her, the Poor

Clares. This spiritual fecundity will not end there because Francis, once again in the Rieti valley, on meeting the Blessed Lucchese of Poggio Bustone, will found a Third Order of those who remain in the secular world whilst professing their faith in Christ and wishing to follow Francis in taking up the Way of the Cross.

In the succeeding three days we will look more specifically at the Franciscan charism in the aspect of its Catholicism, its feminine side and the Way of the Cross, but for the moment I want to continue with some of the essential characteristics of the charism through the lens of the places where Francis lived.

The first of these is San Damiano where Francis heard the call from the cross, where he subsequently took refuge, hiding from his father and where he stayed with the priest, working with his hands and begging the stones for the rebuilding of the church. It is the crucial example of Francis putting the Word into practice. A saying attributed to the Saint, is that the friars should go out to preach the Gospel and only if necessary use words, and whereas this is not written down anywhere, in that order in the sources it is a distillation of the Franciscan spirit and in line what Francis did actually advise. When he did use words, they were prophetic ones. When, one day, he was working on the rebuilding of the church, he called out in French to a group of people passing to come and help because ladies would come to live here whose fame would be known throughout the world. Of course, the prophecy was fulfilled by the arrival of St Clare and her sisters there some years later. After San Damiano, Francis would live in community with brothers at Rivotorto where again the prophetic element came to the fore with one of the brothers seeing him in a vision, like Elijah, in a chariot of fire.

Francis, however, if he had a stable residence anywhere on earth, it was at the Portiuncola — the little portion of land where the church of Our Lady of the Angels stood, and which Francis

The Franciscan Charism

described as the place which was most dear to her and the place which he loved above all others in the world. It was the birthplace of the Order, the place from where the first twelve brothers set out to obtain approval for their Order from the Pope and the place from where all Franciscan missions started. The Franciscan Order was a novelty in that it diverged from previous forms of monastic life with its lack of *stabilitas*. Francis had asked early on for St Clare and the first priest to join the Order, Fr Sylvester, to pray about what he should do. The answers to their prayers concurred — he was not to keep the treasure to himself but to go and spread it throughout the world. Francis replied then that the world is the friar's cloister. But the friars had to have a friary to come back to and the Portiuncola provided the focal point of the Order. At the start, two friars may have been sent north, two south, two east and two west, but each time they came back with other men who wished to join them. In the twelve years from the founding of the Order in 1209, the original group of twelve would swell in 1221 to five thousand. The friars would reach most parts of Europe before the death of Francis in 1226, and the desire to spread the Gospel far and wide continued thereafter with a friar to be found in the court of the Khan in the 1240s, long before Marco Polo, and Spanish speaking friars found in the far West in the sixteenth century led by St Junipero Serra.

Wherever the friars went, however, the essential characteristic was of identifying with the poor and marginalised. This derives from the origins of the Franciscan Order. Midway between the Portiuncola and the town of Rivotorto, the little churches of St Rufinuccio and St Mary Magdalene, which date back to the time of St Francis, are to be found. They were churches around which the respectively male and female leper communities resided. It was here where the brothers went to work to assist the lepers in their illness. The lepers were least in the society of their day, but the friars came and worked amongst them, not for their own gain

Living with St Francis

as penitents, but treating them as brothers and sisters and rendering them service in line with the name Francis gave the friars as 'lesser brothers', Friars Minor. It is this minority that brings us closest to Christ who, as St Paul declares, did not consider his equality with God something to be grasped, but rather abasing himself he became obedient even to death, death on a cross. The basest thing that Francis had come across, and which he was terrified of becoming, was a leper. It was exactly the contrary of everything that he had desired to be as a youth, namely a handsome, rich and noble knight. As Francis describes it in his Testament, however, the great conversion in his life occurred precisely as a result of his encounter with Christ — in this distressing disguise.

> While I was in sin, it seemed very bitter to me to see lepers. And the Lord Himself led me among them and I had mercy upon them. And when I left them, that which seemed bitter to me was changed into sweetness of soul and body; and afterwards I lingered a little and left the world.

The Friar Minor therefore always looks up to people and never down upon them and the example was given from the very start by the founder of the Order.

I conclude this chapter, however, with a look at the Franciscan attitude to creation and the locus for this would be the garden of the Canticle of the Creatures, beside the church of San Damiano where St Francis composed the majority of the poem which bears the same name, in 1225, in the year before his death. The poem can be described also as a prayer, but in it Francis does not ask for anything but simply sings the praise of God through his creation. Francis sees all of God's creation as brothers and sisters from the sun, the moon and the stars, to the earth, wind, fire and water, concluding, however, with those who embrace forgiveness and peace and Sister Death. It is perhaps remarkable that the patron saint of animals does not make any reference to them in this *Canticle*, but his attitude to them is shown throughout his life and reflects a consistent thought, expressed by this poem, that all of creation is the praise God through whatever nature He has bestowed upon them. Thus, when he famously preaches to the birds at Bevagna, the substance is that they should be grateful to God for the feathers he has given to clothe them, the wings that He has given them to allow them to fly, and all that is necessary for them to live. He refers to the Gospel saying that they neither sow nor reap, yet God feeds them, and they need not worry. The birds indeed seem to respond to his preaching and presence, stretching their necks, opening their beaks and flapping their wings here, and on other occasions coming to salute him when he arrives at the mountain of La Verna, or at the hour of his death when the larks fly around him at evening, a time when they are not normally to be seen. Francis also attracts quadrupeds to him, from the sheep that follows him around the Portiuncola, to the leveret that jumps into his lap, and there is, of course, the famous story of the taming of the wolf of Gubbio. But the fascination with the Saint extends also to the insect world, and there is the cicada who joins in the singing of the friars' praises, flying into Francis' hands at his command and returning to the prayers every day for eight days until he gives the insect leave to depart. And Francis does, of course, have particular respect for the worm — replacing any he found on the roadway back onto the earth — because Scripture refers to his Lord as being a worm and no man. Thus, from the great Brother Sun to the humble worm, Francis has something to say. His charism is universal.

Concluding prayer

Response: **Give us the holy virtues, Lord.**

I greet you O Majestic Wisdom;
may the Lord save you with your sister
the pure and holy Simplicity. /R

I greet you O Lady, Holy Poverty;
may the Lord save you with your sister
holy Humility. /R

I greet you O Lady, Holy Charity;
may the Lord save you with your sister
holy Obedience. /R

O all you most holy virtues, may the Lord
from whom you all originate and proceed,
save you through Christ Our Lord. Amen. /R

Day Five

A Truly Catholic Man

Invocation of the Holy Spirit

Come Holy Spirit,
fill the hearts of your faithful
light up in them the fire of your love.

Send your Spirit and all is created.
Renew the face of the earth.

Let us pray:

O God, you have instructed your faithful,
illuminating their hearts with the light of the Holy Spirit.
Grant that we may have in the same Spirit
the taste for goodness,
and enjoy forever his comfort.
Through Christ, our Lord. Amen.

Living with St Francis

The attraction to Francis may be described as catholic, in the sense of universal, as we have seen in the previous chapter. Here in Assisi I have seen visitors from all parts of the world, of nearly all religions and none. Some people simply are attracted to the saint who loved animals, others see an affinity with their own attitudes and beliefs whether they be New Age, Hindu, Muslim or Buddhist. It is not surprising that the now canonised Pope John Paul II chose Assisi to invite leaders of all the religions to celebrate a World Day of Peace in the town in 1986, and many religious leaders returned to commemorate the 25th anniversary of that event hosted by Pope Benedict XVI, his successor. Francis is also esteemed by many other Christian churches, from Lutheran Protestant to High Church Anglican — there is also a society of Anglican brothers who wear the Franciscan habit. This may suggest to someone who has not read the Franciscan sources that Francis' beliefs were syncretistic and diverged somewhat from the teaching of the Catholic Church. Indeed, the impression given in some books and screen adaptations of his life is that he was an attractive revolutionary and an antithesis to the established Church. But nothing could be further from the truth and in this chapter we will look at the writings which show Francis to be a 'truly Catholic man'.

The Order is firmly placed within the hierarchy of the Church — immediately after the opening description of the Franciscan charism in the Rule, there follows the declaration that:

> Brother Francis promises obedience to Pope Honorius and his canonically elected successors and to the Roman Church.
>
> The Approved Rule

And the Catholic nature of the Order is very much underlined in chapter nineteen of the Earlier Rule where Francis declares:

A Truly Catholic Man

All of the friars must be Catholic and live and speak in a Catholic fashion. If someone in words or deed should stray from the Catholic faith and way of life, he should be excluded from our brotherhood.

I think it is useful to see how this Catholicism is well and truly anchored in the history of Franciscanism from the very start. Francis was not only particular about his reverence and obedience to the Pope but he also showed the same respect to bishops and other clergy. As is seen, he did not wish to preach in a diocese — that of Imola is mentioned in the *Second Life of Celano* — without the permission of the bishop, and always wished to have recourse to the clergy of the Catholic Church, even if they were to persecute him. In the same place he says that even if he had the wisdom of Solomon he would not wish to preach in a parish without the consent of the poor priest there. The emphasis on correct Catholic doctrine comes through at every point.

Perhaps this is clearest in his *Letter to the Faithful* (second version), which Francis writes as a servant of all who is called to administer 'the fragrant words of my Lord', words which are 'spirit and life'. There is reference immediately to an angel — the spirits for whom Francis had a particular devotion as our allies in the field of battle, especially the Archangel Michael in whose honour he fasted each year for forty days, and the Virgin Mary in whom he rejoiced, singing songs, hymns and offices of praise, and whom he called Advocate of the Order. Various encouragements to the faithful to follow Catholic precepts follow as can be seen from the quotations below:

Let us love God therefore and adore Him with a pure heart and a pure mind.

Let us praise Him and pray to Him day and night, saying 'Our Father who art in heaven'.

Living with St Francis

> We must confess all our sins to a priest and receive from
> him the Body and Blood of our Lord Jesus Christ.
>
> Let us then have charity and humility; let us give alms
> since this washes our souls from the stains of sin.
>
> We must also fast and abstain from vices and sins and
> from any excess of food and drink and be Catholics. We
> must also visit churches frequently and show respect for
> the clergy, not so much for them personally if they are
> sinners, but by reason of their office and their
> administration of the most holy Body and Blood of
> Christ which they sacrifice upon the altar and receive and
> administer to others. And let all of us firmly realise, that
> no one can be saved except through the holy words and
> Blood of our Lord Jesus Christ, which the clergy
> pronounce, proclaim and minister. And they alone must
> administer them and not others.

There is also an encouragement to religious, who have left the
world, for them to do not alone these things but much more and
greater things, as their duty.

What stands out perhaps most is Francis' love for the Word of
God and the Eucharist. These holy mysteries, as he writes in his
Testament, are to be honoured and venerated in precious places —
Francis underlines his desire that the precious words are held in
decorous places and that theologians are respected and honoured.
This respect and honour to the sacred mysteries, particularly the
Eucharist, is repeated several times in his writings, for example, in
the *Letter to the Clergy*, the *Letter to Custodians* and the *Letter to the Entire
Order*. In the last-mentioned, Francis expresses himself thus:

> Therefore, kissing your feet and with all the love of which
> I am capable, I implore all of you brothers to show all

possible reverence and honour to the most holy Body and
Blood of our Lord Jesus Christ.

In the *Admonitions* it is the first topic that he deals with and, in
terms of length, by far the longest. Francis compares the
condemnation of those who did not accept Jesus as the Son of
God, seeing Him in the body, with those who see the sacrament
and do not believe it is the Body and Blood of our Lord Jesus
Christ. His belief in the doctrine of transubstantiation is
poetically expressed in that first admonition.

> See daily He humbles Himself as when he came down
> from the royal throne into the womb of the Virgin; daily
> He comes to us in a humble form; daily He comes down
> from the bosom of the Father upon the altar in the hands
> of the priest. And as he appeared to the holy apostles in
> true flesh, so now He reveals Himself to us in the sacred
> bread.

I have quoted the sources at length, but far from exhaustively, to
demonstrate the regard in which Francis held the Catholic
Church, its teachings and how he viewed his place in it. He
looked to Rome as his guide from the very origins of the Order,
when he walked to the city with his twelve followers to obtain
approval from the Pope for his religion, as he called it. He sought
support from the hierarchy of the Church in terms of a cardinal
who would be a protector of the Order and used the Roman
breviary to direct the prayer life of his friars. He was clearly a son
of the Church and although he saw the faults and sins of the
people in it, he was called to rebuild it spiritually. He recalled
priests to their dignity, kissing the hands of sinful priests who
then repented, and acted strongly against friars who showed
themselves not to be Catholic by their conduct, dismissing them
from the Order. This may have been because they left the other

friars to do their work, such as one friar who Francis nicknamed Brother Fly, or for the serious sin of fornication as referred to in the Rule. The image, which perhaps shows most figuratively Francis' relationship with the Church, is that of Giotto's fresco, to be found in the Basilica of St Francis in Assisi, which depicts the dream of Pope Innocent III who saw the figure of the friar holding up the falling Lateran Cathedral. Francis is not supporting the edifice from the outside, his feet are planted within the building. His was not a pauperist movement which criticised the Church from the outside.

Francis was thus an integral part of the Church. A body that was distinctly female in its characteristics. The spouse of Jesus, the one for whom He gave his life; the Mother who loved her children and cleansed them from the iniquity of sin, and the daughter of the Most High God, the Father Almighty. It is not surprising to discover then that the Order which Francis founded should reflect this feminine side at the very centre of its charism, and that is what we shall look at next.

Concluding prayer

Response: **Holy Father, guard in your name those you have given me.**

Oh, how glorious, holy and great
it is to have a Father in heaven!
Oh how holy, full of consolation, beautiful and admirable
to have such a Spouse! /R

How holy, how delicious,
how pleasant, humble, peaceful, sweet, loveable,
and above everything desirable,

A Truly Catholic Man

to have such a brother and such a Son,
Our Lord Jesus Christ,
who offers his life for his sheep,
and prays to the Father for us, saying: /R

'Holy Father, Guard in your name
those you have given me in the world:
they were yours and you gave them to me.
And the words you gave to me I have given to them
and they have accepted them
and have truly recognised that I came from you
and they have believed that you sent me. /R

I pray for them and not for the world.
Bless them and make them holy!
And for them I sanctify myself
because they may be made holy in unity as we are. /R

And I wish Father
that where I am so they may also be,
so that they may contemplate my glory in your kingdom.'
Amen. /R

DAY SIX

THE FEMININE SIDE

Invocation of the Holy Spirit

Come Holy Spirit, come into our hearts
with your great power draw them to you.
Grant us charity with fear of you.
Warm us, inflame us with your most sweet love.
Let it be that every suffering seems light to us.
O sweet Father, O sweet Lord,
help us now in what we do.
Christ love, Christ love, Christ love.

Adapted from a prayer of St Catherine of Siena

The immediate thought that springs to mind when bringing up
the subject of the feminine side of Franciscanism is St Clare and
the Second Order, the Poor Clares. Perhaps, then, one would go
on to look at the various Third Order congregations to see how
this feminine side developed in a multitude of ways. However, I
wish to start by looking at the 'feminine' side of St Francis. This
may seem a contradiction in terms but the striking thing about

Living with St Francis

Francis was how he looked at the nature of woman and her role in unifying a society — and how he took that as a model to be followed. In the centre of his Rule, he writes:

> And let each one confidently make known his need to the other, for, if a mother has such care and love for her son born according to the flesh, should not someone love and care for his brother according to the Spirit even more diligently?

He also referred to himself as a mother — in his letter to Brother Leo he writes, 'I speak to you, my son, as a mother.' In his dreams he recognised himself as the beautiful poor woman who had many children by a King who recognises them, when they come to court, to be of his blood. He is also called mother by Brother Pacifico, and selects Brother Elias, the Minister General who was to succeed him, to be 'mother' for himself. Even St Clare, in a dream recounted by her sisters at the process that led to her canonisation, envisaged Francis as a mother who fed her.

Perhaps the most striking feature of Francis' writings on this aspect is the *Rule for Hermitages* which highlights and esteems the characteristics of feminine spirituality. At its very beginning the feminine nature of this way of life is stated:

> Those who wish to live religiously in hermitages should be three brothers or four at the most; two of these should be mothers and they may have two children or at least one. The two who are mothers should follow the life of Martha, while the two children should follow the life of Mary.

Taking the example of the two sisters in the Gospel who were friends of Jesus, Francis points the way to the ideal of contemplative life in the community. The brother who takes on

The Feminine Side

the role of Mary should not be distracted in any way from listening to the words of the Lord, which is the better part, whilst the brothers act as mothers looking after the physical and even spiritual need of silence for their brother/child. This is made clear later in the second part of the *Rule for Hermitages*.

> Those brothers who are mothers should be eager to stay away from every person; and because of their obedience to their minister they should protect their sons from everyone, so that no one can talk with them.

The idea of the mother for Francis is of someone who is beautiful — the poor beautiful woman in the desert who attracted and married a king, referred to above; who is fertile — she has many children; who is caring and protective, as can be seen from the above quotation. Perhaps the care and protection he had received from his own mother, when she had released him from the chains in which his father kept him, reinforced his sensibility to the importance of motherhood. It is important to note that the adoption of the roles by the brothers in the hermitages was not a permanent one and the brothers would interchange their roles from time to time as 'it seems good to them', which is made clear at the end of this particular Rule.

After considering this feminine aspect of Francis and the First Order we can turn now to the representative of the purely feminine side of Franciscanism, St Clare, and the Second Order. St Clare was a young noblewoman from Assisi whose good works Francis had heard of when he became a friar. I think it is fair to say that he targeted her as an object of his preaching — referring to her as 'a noble prey' — and she became, just as he was, an ardent follower of Jesus, poor and crucified. Francis was obviously a role model for Clare, and Clare a special disciple for Francis but it is important to put their relationship in the context of the times in which they were living. Firstly, they begin as enemies. Clare and her aristocratic family are driven out of Assisi by the revolt of the middle class who rise up against the nobles in 1198. Francis is on the side of the same middle class of Assisi as an armed soldier in the battle of Collestrada in 1202. It is the noble class who hold him for ransom in the prison of Perugia. When Francis converted and began his 'religion' it is clear from his writings and the sources that he regarded religious sisters as spouses of God, and he would not even look at the face of a holy virgin who came to assist him with her mother when he was in need. Similarly, he forbade friars other than chaplains to enter into the convents of the sisters in the Rule and directed that no friar was ever to take a female under obedience. Yet he did impart the form of life which the sisters should follow. It is described in simple terms as 'daughters and handmaids of the Most High King, the Heavenly Father, and spouses of the Holy Spirit choosing to live according to the perfection of the Holy Gospel' (Writings to Clare of Assisi). Again, in exactly the same way as the friars, he counsels the Poor Ladies of San Damiano to always live in this most holy life and poverty and never to stray away from it. Francis also declared that he and his friars would have care and special solicitude for the sisters, and he does this by allowing the friars to go and beg the supplies necessary for the sisters to live.

If Francis came to symbolise another Christ for the First Order, so Clare came to represent the Virgin Mary in terms of the Second Order. This can even be seen in terms of the artworks in the respective Basilicas dedicated to the saints. In the Lower Basilica of St Francis the frescoes on one side of the *via sacra* leading to the main altar depict scenes from the life of Francis and scenes from the life of Christ on the other; whilst the same relationship can be discerned in the frescoes that remain in St Clare's Basilica with depictions from the Saint's life in one transept and Mary's on the opposite one. And the role of the Poor

The Feminine Side

Clares, just as Mary at the feast of Cana, is to intercede with Christ for the needs of the humanity with whom they come in touch, even in their enclosed state, and to advise the people to follow the Lord's commands. The role of the sisters was summed up by an ex-Provincial here in terms of their prayer — as being the lungs of the Franciscan movement. It is the contemplative life and prayer which particularly characterises the Second Order and the value of that is inestimable, just as the worth of the Mother of God herself. It is not perhaps surprising that Clare's death is marked by the visit of the Virgin Mary, the model of all disciples, and most particularly Clare's model. She describes her as the sweetest mother in the following terms in her third letter to St Agnes of Prague:

> The sun and the moon admire her beauty,
> her rewards are of infinite value and worth.
> I mean the Son of the Most High
> to whom the Virgin gave birth,
> without ceasing to be a virgin.
> Hold tightly to his sweetest Mother
> who gave birth to such a Son,
> who the Heavens were not able to contain,
> yet she welcomed Him in the little cloister of her breast,
> and bore Him in her virginal womb.
> You too, following in her footsteps,
> and especially in His humility and poverty,
> can always, without any shadow of doubt,
> bear Him spiritually in your body.
> And you will possess that which is more enduringly
> and definitively good in comparison with all of the
> wealth of this world.
>
> From the Prayers of St Clare

The feminine aspects of the Franciscan charism are not exhausted by the first two Orders but appear strongly in the Third Order as well. Francis conceived of this lay Order for those who wished to follow his teaching of poverty, but who were bound by their responsibilities of married and family life in the world. Merchants, like the blessed Lucchese of Poggibonsi, and nobility, such as King Louis IX of France and St Elizabeth of Hungary were among the early followers of St Francis in the Third Order, as well as the famous poet Dante Alighieri. The Third Order developed throughout the ages, however, and even became partially clericalised with the introduction of fraternities such as the Third Order Regulars and latterly the Society of Friars of the Atonement, which accentuates the importance of Christian Unity and works much in the field of ecumenism. These fraternities have their female religious branches and apart from those there are numerous female religious congregations who take as their guide the Rule of the Third Order of St Francis. Such sisters assist, for example, in welcoming pilgrims to Franciscan sanctuaries, collaborate in the missions of the Friars and their pastoral work, as well as working directly with the poor and marginalised in society. Women are also generally in the majority of the Secular Franciscan Order groups that are formed in many parishes throughout the world and the importance of the feminine input cannot be under-estimated or undervalued. The example again comes from the Virgin Mary who points the way to Christ and the love of such women as St Mary Magdalene, the first apostle of the resurrection, who remained in tears searching for her Lord when other apostles had gone away. That particularly feminine love is perhaps best expressed by St Clare in her fourth letter to St Agnes of Prague, where she poetically expresses her love for Christ in the prayer, 'Draw me to you!'

> Contemplate the unspeakable love
> with which He wished to suffer upon the wood of the cross
> and on it to die the most infamous of deaths.
> So that from the height of the cross

The Feminine Side

a voice is directed towards the passers-by
in order that they may stop to consider:
'O all of you, who pass by upon this road,
stop and judge if there is sorrow comparable to mine.'
And we will reply to Him who calls and groans,
with one voice and one heart:
'Your memory will never depart from me
and my soul will be consumed.'
Contemplate then His unutterable delights
His wealth and eternal honours,
and shout ardently
with all your love and all your desire:
'Draw me to yourself, O Heavenly Spouse!
We will run after you drawn by the sweetness of your perfume.'

From the Prayers of St Clare

Concluding prayer

Response: **I salute you Holy Lady, Most Holy Queen, Mary, Mother of God.**

You are the Virgin, made Church.
You are the chosen one of our Most Holy Heavenly Father. /R

By Him consecrated with his delightful Most Holy Son
and with the Holy Spirit Advocate,
you had and have every fullness of grace and every good. /R

I salute you, his palace and his tabernacle,
his raiment and his house, his handmaid and his mother. /R

And I salute you all holy virtues,
which through the grace and enlightenment of the Holy Spirit
are infused into the hearts of the faithful,
so that from unfaithful they are made faithful unto God. /R

Day Seven

The Way of the Cross

Invocation of the Holy Spirit

Come, O Holy Spirit, and give us a new heart
that revives in us all the gifts received from you
with the joy of being Christians;
a new heart always youthful and joyous.

Come, O Holy Spirit,
and give us a pure heart trained to love God;
a pure heart that does not know evil,
except in knowing how to define it,
to combat it and make it flee;
a pure heart like that of a child
capable of feeling enthusiasm and trepidation.

Come, O Holy Spirit, and give us a great heart
open to your silent and powerful inspiring Word,
and closed to every craven ambition,
a heart that is great and strong, capable of loving everyone,
of serving everyone and of suffering with everyone,

Living with St Francis

a heart that is great, strong and blessed,
to be able to beat with the heart of God.

Pope St Paul VI

> If anyone would come after me let him take up his cross
> and follow me. For whoever would save his life will lose
> it, and whoever loses his life for my sake will find it.

Matthew 16: 24–25

It is a paradox that the uniquely Christian emblem — the cross —
is an instrument of torture and death in this world but an
indispensable key to finding eternal life in the next, according to
the words of Christ cited above. In looking at Franciscan
spirituality in relation to the cross, there is perhaps no better way
than commencing with the prayer of Francis on La Verna which
precedes his vision and subsequent reception of the stigmata:

> O my Lord Jesus Christ, two graces I beg of you before I
> die: the first that whilst I live I may feel in my soul and
> in my body, insofar as it is possible, that pain which you
> sweet Jesus, sustained in the hour of your most bitter
> passion: the second that I may feel in my heart, insofar as
> it is possible, that excessive love with which you, Son of
> God, were inflamed to sustain such suffering voluntarily
> for us sinners.

The Little Flowers of St Francis

The prayer was heard and answered in the subsequent vision of
the Crucified Seraphim who imprinted the stigmata upon the
body of Francis, the two sides of the prayer blending into his
experience, as the words of St Bonaventure in the *Legenda Maior*
indicate:

The Way of the Cross

> He experienced joy for the gentle way in which he was looked upon by Christ in the form of the Seraphim; but to see Him nailed to the cross sent a sword through [Francis'] heart and pained him with compassion.

The Franciscan cross is the Tau. You could say that it is literally woven into the fabric of Franciscans. The habit we wear is in the form of the Tau, the sign that Francis loved. I think that it is important to note that Francis always returned to the word of God when he sought to pass on things of worth to his fellow friars. He sought the guidance of the Gospel in respect of adopting his missionary charism — or possibly the liturgy, since the reading may have been taken from a missal. His blessing on Brother Leo is essentially that of Numbers 6:24–26:

> May the Lord bless you and keep you. May He show his face to you and be merciful to you. May He turn His countenance towards you and give you peace. May the Lord bless you, Brother Leo.

Similarly, he goes back to the Old Testament in respect of the Tau which is the sign placed on the foreheads by the Angel to protect those to be saved from destruction. Francis loved this sign and painted it on the cells where he resided. He also signed the parchment given to Brother Leo with this mark — the parchment which is to be found in St Francis' Basilica at present. As it is at the centre of this parchment it is also at the centre of the first common prayer of the fraternity — again a slight variation on a typically Catholic prayer:

> We adore you, O Christ, here and in all the churches throughout the world, and we bless you, because by your holy cross you have redeemed the world.
>
> Testament of St Francis

Living with St Francis

What is the cross then? It could be described as the epitome of one's personal fears. To be stripped, beaten, spat upon and derided and then nailed to a cross to die in the most ignominious and painful way possible, could be possibly described as many people's worst nightmare. For this to be done when the person treated this way has only done good, and never evil, appears to be the height of injustice. But paradoxically it is God's justice and righteousness. Francis confronts his worst nightmare on the day when he embraces that which he most fears. It was for him too bitter an event to behold a leper but, as he says, the Lord himself led him among them and he used mercy towards them. It is interesting how he continues with the story:

> And going away from them, that which seemed bitter to me was changed into sweetness of soul and body. Then I stayed for a little while and then I left the world.
>
> Testament of St Francis

As the footnote in the Franciscan sources pertaining to the last phrase in this sentence points out, the 'leaving of the world' usually meant going into a monastery, but for Francis it had above all a spiritual significance and meant his determination to consecrate himself totally to God's service.

I think it is fair to say that the embracing of the leper was not a one-off incident which thereupon made everything easy for Francis. It was something that he perhaps then did every day, embracing that which to others may have been repugnant and thereby changing the situation radically in a manner that could not have been foreseen. A number of examples spring to mind, such as the story of the three brigands. The tale is recounted in the *Little Flowers of St Francis* and relates how a friar, who was a young guardian, encounters three men who are infamous for their ways as brigands and robbers and are asking to be fed by the friars. He reproves them harshly, asking them if they are not

The Way of the Cross

ashamed to come asking for the alms given to servants of God when they have no respect for man or God and are murderers and cruel robbers. However, Francis on his return to the friary rebukes the guardian severely, citing the way Jesus was kind to sinners and ate with them. He sends the friar after the brigands to beg their pardon and sends them a present of some bread and wine that he has begged. The friar does precisely that, kneeling down and confessing his fault before them and leaving them the gift of St Francis. As they eat they become remorseful of their previous life and ask themselves if this holy friar should consider it a fault to have justly reproved them for their way of life, how can they be saved? They seek out Francis for guidance and, as a result of what he tells them, they not only convert but enter into the brotherhood as friars. Their leader, who was nicknamed 'Wolf', takes the name of 'Brother Lamb'! Similarly, we remember how Francis does not threaten, menace or condemn the beautiful woman who is attempting to seduce him but shows her the error of her ways, inviting to her to a bed where she cannot possibly lie down, and kisses the hands of the sinful priest. Francis embraces what is difficult in life and changes it; he does not let evil overcome good but overcomes evil through his good acts. Not only does he overcome it; he transforms the situation completely. The thorn bush he jumps into becomes a rosebush without thorns; the 'place of the evil eye' becomes the Hermitage of the Carceri, the hill in Assisi which was used for executions turns from being the hill of Hell to the hill of Paradise. Francis accepts his cross and finds that it turns from an instrument of torture to the tree of life.

It is on this positive message that I wish to finish our time with St Francis. When joining the friars it was impressed upon me that the crucifixion of Jesus could never be separated from his resurrection. Because, although for a little while the followers of Jesus had to grieve his loss, the joy that ensued upon his

Living with St Francis

resurrection was a joy that could not be taken away. Francis, on a cold and miserable day walking back to the Portiuncola from Perugia, described to Friar Masseo what perfect joy consisted in. It involved suffering cold and hunger and maltreatment, unjust rejection by one's brothers and the acceptance of that without protest. Enduring with patience and conquering yourself is the very essence of perfect joy. What is promised thereafter in the Second Letter of St Peter are new heavens and a new earth in which righteousness shall be at home. Hints of that heavenly country come from creation as we presently see it but our desires will be fulfilled when we hear the voice that calls us to enter into his kingdom. This is the theme of the poem *Portami il Sole* (Bring me the sun) which I translate below:

> Bring me the sun, that is what is needed.
> A ray of golden light to warm to the very heart.
>
> Bring me the moon which reflects your wondrous beauty,
> a gleam of silver in a river, the very symbol of love.
>
> Bring me the stars, little mirrors of that life
> that now grow within you and will very soon be born.
>
> 'Come!' He is saying, 'Come and do not hold back.
> Come now and drink from this cool refreshing spring.'
>
> Now can you not hear the voice of your Beloved
> calling you to taste from the fount of everlasting joy!

It is the voice that we all long to hear: a voice of joy, a voice of peace, a voice of love. A voice for eternity — to which Francis points.

Concluding prayer

Response: **To fulfil your will is our great consolation, Lord.**

O Lord Jesus Christ,
two graces I beg you to grant me before I die.
The first, that in my life I may feel in my soul and in my body,
insofar as it is possible, the pain that you, sweet Jesus,
suffered in the hour of your most bitter Passion. /**R**

The second, that I feel in my heart, insofar as it is possible,
that great love, with which you, Son of God, were ablaze
to willingly sustain such a Passion for us poor sinners. /**R**

PORTAMI IL SOLE

Portami il sole è la cosa che ci vuole
un raggio di luce che faccia caldo fino al cuore.
Portami la luna che rifletta il tuo splendore,
una luce in un fiume, il simbolo d'amore.
Portami le stelle, piccoli specchi della vita
che cresce dentro di te e sarà ben presto partorita.

'Vieni', Lui dice, 'e non essere titubante.
Vieni qui e bevi del rampollo rinfrescante.'
Or non puoi sentire la sua voce amata
che ti chiama a provare la gioia sconfinata.

Sources

The Franciscan references throughout this book come almost exclusively from Italian texts which have been translated by the author. The first of these, the Franciscan Sources, is a compilation of all the writings of both St Francis and St Clare, the biographies and chronicles of their stories.

The Franciscan Sources
Fonti Francescane (Editrice Francescane, 2011)

Prayers of the Fraternity
Le Preghiere della Fraternità (Edizioni Porziuncola, 2006)

The Franciscan Rosary
Il Rosario Francescano (Edizioni Porziuncola, 2011)

The Prayers of St Clare
Le Preghiere di Santa Chiara (Edizioni Porziuncola, 2006)

G. K. Chesterton, *St. Francis of Assisi* (London: Hodder & Stoughton, 1944)

The Sayings of Blessed Giles
I Detti di Frate Egidio: Beato Egidio di Assisi (Le Vie della Cristianità, 2016)

Camilla Battista da Varano: The Spiritual Life and Other Writings, trans. by William V. Hudson from the Italian, *La Vita Spirituale e altre opere: Santa Camilla Battista da Varano* (University of Chicago Press, 2023)